WHAT I'VE LEARNED THROUGH TRIALS AND TRIBULATIONS

T.K WARE and Special Guests

Copyright © 2021 by Tshombye K. Ware

All rights reserved. No part of this publication may be reproduced, distributed, or transmitted in any form or by any means, including photocopying, recording, or other electronic or mechanical methods, without the prior written permission of the publisher, except in the case of brief quotations embodied in critical reviews and certain other noncommercial uses permitted by copyright law.

Printed in the United States of America

First Printing, 2021
ISBN: 9781638211389

Insightful Creation Publication
We INSPIRE to INSPIRE
www.insightfulcp.com
services@insightfulcp.com

Ordering Information: Special discounts are available on quantity purchases by corporations, associations, and others. For details, contact the publisher at the email address above.

1 Peter 5:10 But the God of all grace, who hath called us unto his eternal glory by Christ Jesus, after that ye have suffered a while, make you perfect, stablish, strengthen, settle you.

OTHER BOOKS

FICTION
If I Could: A Son's Plea
A Husband's Love
WEB OF ALLURE
WEB OF ALLURE: The Entrapment
The Pastor's Daughter
Ebony's Confessions
Memory Iota
Portent of Eternity
The Letters of Warning
Caveat of Penitent
THRESHOLD

ESQUIRE SERIES
Trial of INJUSTICE
ESQUIRE: THE LAWYER OF FAITH
Theodore Esquire: The Protégé
Theodore Esquire: The Trial
ESQUIRE: The Appeal
ESQUIRE: The Summon

NON FICTION
21 Day Journey of Inspiration
Battling & Overcoming Self
GOD doesn't condemn you, Neither do I
Run the Race: 50 Days of Inspiration
Utilizing Your Gifts to Advance the Kingdom
THE POWER OF BELIEF
THE POWER OF WORDS
THE POWER OF FORGIVENESS

THE POWER OF DELIVERANCE
Been there, done that
The Process of Waiting
Hello Queen
Queen 2 Queen
MAN UP
The Journey of Discovery
Keep Going, It's Not Over
Fret Not, It's The Same Power
Inward Search of Hope
TIME DRAWETH NIGH
Your Circumstance is Just a STANCE for His GLORY

<u>POETRY</u>
TRIUMPH
Soul Writings
The Writings of Epiphany
Poet Talk
Our KING Lives

CHILDREN BOOKS
I Can and I Will
Positive Declarations for Children

Dedication
To those with a love for God

Scriptures about overcoming Trials and Tribulations

- ❖ James 1:12 Blessed is the man that endureth temptation: for when he is tried, he shall receive the crown of life, which the Lord hath promised to them that love him.

- ❖ Romans 12:12 Rejoicing in hope; patient in tribulation; continuing instant in prayer;

- ❖ 1 Corinthians 10:13 There hath no temptation taken you but such as is common to man: but God is faithful, who will not suffer you to be tempted above that ye are able; but will with the temptation also make a way to escape, that ye may be able to bear it.

- ❖ John 16:33 These things I have spoken unto you, that in me ye might have peace. In the world ye shall have tribulation: but be of good cheer; I have overcome the world.

- ❖ Exodus 14:14 The LORD shall fight for you, and ye shall hold your peace.

- ❖ Romans 5:3 And not only so, but we glory in tribulations also: knowing that tribulation worketh patience;

- ❖ Psalms 23:4 Yea, though I walk through the valley of the shadow of death, I will fear no evil: for thou [art] with me; thy rod and thy staff they comfort me.

- Romans 8:18 For I reckon that the sufferings of this present time are not worthy to be compared with the glory which shall be revealed in us.

- Hebrews 10:35 Cast not away therefore your confidence, which hath great recompence of reward.

- James 1:2 My brethren, count it all joy when ye fall into divers temptations;

- 1 Peter 4:12 Beloved, think it not strange concerning the fiery trial which is to try you, as though some strange thing happened unto you:

- Philippians 4:13 I can do all things through Christ which strengtheneth me.

- Romans 8:28 And we know that all things work together for good to them that love God, to them who are the called according to his purpose.

- Matthew 19:26 But Jesus beheld [them], and said unto them, With men this is impossible; but with God all things are possible.

- 2 Corinthians 12:9 And he said unto me, My grace is sufficient for thee: for my strength is made perfect in weakness. Most gladly therefore will I rather glory in my infirmities, that the power of Christ may rest upon me.

- ❖ Philippians 4:6-7 Be careful for nothing; but in every thing by prayer and supplication with thanksgiving let your requests be made known unto God.
  [7] And the peace of God, which passeth all understanding, shall keep your hearts and minds through Christ Jesus.

- ❖ Proverbs 3:5-6 Trust in the LORD with all thine heart; and lean not unto thine own understanding.
  [6] In all thy ways acknowledge him, and he shall direct thy paths.

- ❖ Psalms 34: 17-18 The righteous cry, and the LORD heareth, and delivereth them out of all their troubles.
  [18] The LORD is nigh unto them that are of a broken heart; and saveth such as be of a contrite spirit.

WHAT I'VE LEARNED THROUGH TRIALS AND TRIBULATIONS

Table of Contents

Foreword by Apostle L. Spencer Thomas Sr. 17

Introduction 18

Trials and Tribulations by Marlo The Poet McLeod 19

The Process of Growth by T.K. Ware 21

Strength Beyond Trials by Minister Denise Lamar 32

Lesson Learned by Kanonta Haynes 35

Forgiveness Is Greater by Christine L. George 37

What I Learned From My Miscarriage by Shenna M. Ware 41

God's Faithfulness by Linda G. Pugh, MS, NCC, LAPC 46

The Blessings in the Trials by Kim P. Carrol 52

Perseverance by Tra' Derrius Robinson 55

Purpose with a plan by Que Nona Guilford 58

Trust the Process by Kim J. McKinney 61

About the Author 67

Journal Entries 68

THE NAMES OF JESUS 84

VISION: THE EYES OF POET(COMING SO0N)Positioning For The Future 103

Foreword
by Apostle L. Spencer Thomas

When you're going through the trials and tribulations of life and the Christian walk, we must remind ourselves that these are the **WORKINGS** of the Lord to establish in us:

- ❖ OUR TESTING(validation of our LOVE for GOD to US)

- ❖ OUR BANNER(a proven stand on the WORD of GOD)

- ❖ OUR MIRACLE(GOD'S WORKINGS beyond OUR EXPLANATION)

We cannot explain the trials and tribulations but at the end, we know **GOD HAD US** and He **GOT US RIGHT NOW!**

James 5:11

Behold, we count them happy which endure. Ye have heard of the patience of Job, and have seen the end of the Lord; that the Lord is very pitiful, and of tender mercy.

Introduction

In WHAT I'VE LEARNED THROUGH TRIALS AND TRIBULATIONS, T.K.WARE and a host of like-minded individuals share jewels of knowledge and wisdom obtained through life experiences.

A potent concept echoed throughout the book is that JESUS WILL NEVER FAIL. Trials and tribulations will arise in your life, but the Word of God is absolute, and it will sustain you. The LORD is not thinking evil about you. If you turn your mind toward Him, there is a pathway of expectation preordained just for you! Go beyond living in defeat and walk in the newness of life.

Trials and Tribulations
by Marlo The Poet McLeod

Trials and tribulations are the things that can either make you or break you
They can hold you back or move you forward
They can keep you stuck and stagnant or help you open the flood gates of heavens
They can be your downfall or your uplifter
With every blow I took,
every bruise I wore
every scar
I'm healing from my trials and tribulations
they brought me closer to God
With the gun pointed to my head
not knowing if it would go off
I cried out to the only person who would hear my cries
God
When my child got taken away for capital murder
I leaned not on my own understanding
but that of God's
I fasted
I prayed
I knew the trails and tribulations
that my son and I faced

was going to either make us fall and not get up
or let us leap for joy
because our God says,
the righteous fall seven times but rises up again
On the day, my son got released
I cried out with joy to God
knowing had it not been for Him on our side
my son would have been another statistic lost in the system
My trials and tribulations still hold scars
but they are good scars.
Scars of not giving up
Scars of being a survivor
Scars of being an overcomer
Scars of hope and love
And scars of my faith in God

So now the question is what will you do when you're faced with your own trails and tribulations?

The Process of Growth
by T.K. Ware

Never take your life for granted. It is a precious gift manifested by the glory of God. He alone is the life-giver. Before the foundations of the world, He declared and designed a path of expectation for those who would enter the gateway of faith. If you can believe, there is a plan of EXPECTATION for you!

Jeremiah 29:11 says, "For I know the thoughts that I think toward you, saith the LORD, thoughts of peace, and not of evil, to give you an expected end."

This passage means you don't have to figure out which path to take in life. Simply trust the guidance of the Lord. Just trust the Designer of life. You are wonderfully made by an Almighty God! Every day is an opportunity to bask in the goodness of the Lord. Our King is worthy of all praises!

In spite of what our lives or our world may look like, God is still in control. His rule is Sovereign, and He makes no mistakes. Does His sovereignty mean your life will be filled with roses? No, it doesn't.

Psalms 34:19 says, "Many are the afflictions of the righteous: but the LORD delivereth him out of them all."

Hardship will arise, circumstances will frustrate you, betrayal will occur, misunderstandings will drive wedges between relationships, trials and tribulations will push you to the edge of your faith, and the list goes on and on. Life may be difficult when you're going through a situation because you're viewing it as it is, instead of what it can be.

Hebrews 11:1 says, "Now faith is the substance of things hoped for, the evidence of things not seen."

I remember when the evidence of what I hoped for manifested in a spectacular way. I've learned that if you can envision whatever you're believing God for in your mind, without a shadow of doubt, then according to your faith, it shall manifest in due time.

Now, let me show you what I just said.

When the reputation of my basketball abilities reached the ears of a scout, I was invited to a basketball tournament at a local gym in Macon. When it was my time to perform, I didn't disappoint the scouts. On that particular day, I was a three-point specialist. The more I shot, the more my confidence grew. When the game was settled, I knew I had performed well. A few weeks later, I received a phone call with collegiate offers. I chose the best one, according to my desires. I was excited! I had prayed for the opportunity, and the moment had arrived. Well, I didn't factor in the education part of the process. I simply wanted to go to college to play basketball and didn't consider the working on a degree, housing, and so forth.

When I arrived on the campus, the basketball coach took me around on a tour of the school. Later that afternoon, we had a scrimmage game with the other athletes. Once everything was settled, the basketball coach took me into his office and told me something that rocked my foundation. I had traveled hundreds of miles with no way of return to hear, "I don't have any scholarships available right now, but I will have some next semester."

I could've choked that man. He could've told me this on the phone. I sat there in disbelief and wondered if God was with me. When I attempted to register for classes, the out of state fees and tuition were more than I had. I sought means to obtain the necessary finances but was unable to.

I didn't' know what to do, so I did what I knew best. Trust God. I had no money in my pocket, no scholarship, no financial aid, and the last day to register for classes was less than two days away. One of the basketball players allowed me to stay at his home until I figured out my situation. I was in a tug of war between faith and fear. Fear told me to drive back to Georgia and forget about college, and Faith told me to, "Trust in the Lord with all thine heart; and lean not unto thine own understanding. In all thy ways acknowledge him, and he shall direct thy paths" (Proverbs 3:5-6).

I had almost given into fear, but then I heard in my spirit, "Now faith is the substance of things hoped for, the evidence of things not seen" (Hebrews 11:1).

All of the teachings of faith rushed into my spirit, and flashes of the men and women of God throughout the Bible churned in my soul.

I silenced the screams of fear and mediated on the Word of God.

I awoke early the next morning, got dressed, threw notepads and pens into my book bag, and went back to the campus. No one was there. I didn't know what was going to happen, but I believed that something would happen. I envisioned going to classes and playing on the basketball team. Once my nerves settled, I got out of my truck and walked toward one of the buildings as if I were going to class. With each step I took, the tug of war between faith and fear returned, but I was determined to hold onto my faith. Before I reached the campus door, I turned at the sound of my name. The basketball coach walked up to me and said, "SOMETHING just happened, and a scholarship just BECAME available."

I nodded and followed him into the office, but deep down inside, my soul shouted, "Thank You, Jesus!"

My joy wasn't about the scholarship but for the simple fact that the scripture came to life before me. So it doesn't matter what you're going through, if you believe and hold onto that belief, at the "right time," all things will work together for your good. God is a Master Designer, and He knows what's best for us. Our lives are open before Him and He knows what's best. Every test may not result in what you hope for, but every test is hopeful.

Never charge God foolishly for something that didn't go as you planned. Before I went to college, I was trying to find my way, but the distractions of the city life were alluring me in all types of directions. So God isolated me in an environment, to bring me to a place "in" Him, which would require an increase of my trust in His guidance. So when we're going through trials and tribulations, surrender to the will of the Lord. He knows the beginning, middle, and ending of everything. Nothing just happens. Whatever happens is purposeful, for a particular purpose. He who holds the keys to life and death is mindful and determined to bring you to an expected end.

Moving Beyond Through Trials and Tribulations

To live in the essence of love and stay away from all forms of negativity is critical for everyone. Thanks to the Covid19 pandemic, the year of 2020 will forever be etched in history. So many people have lost loved ones and the list continues to grow. Take a moment and let's pray for all who have been affected.

If you didn't learn anything from the year of 2020, it should be evident that everyone needs to operate in forgiveness and cultivate their relationship with Jesus. This is not the time for slacking or walking around with grudges or unresolved feelings of unforgiveness.

Let them go.

Troublesome times will arise. You may not want to accept that everything is moving toward the 2nd coming of the Messiah, but biblical days are upon the earth. The cosmic stage is strategically aligning for the coming of the Messiah. Now is the time to run into the Ark of Safety while the waves of fear are flowing across the Planet.

Revelation 1:7 *Behold, he cometh with clouds; and every eye shall see him, and they also which pierced him: and all kindreds of the earth shall wail because of him. Even so, Amen.*

May I ask you a few questions?

1. What's hindering you from developing or establishing a relationship with Jesus?
2. Are you afraid that you will be forced to perform certain acts?
3. Are you fearful that you're not quite ready to take the relationship seriously?

Consider those questions and measure where you are. With everything that's happening in the world, the safest place is in the divine will of the Lord. He is your hope through any crisis that may arise. Being in the shelter of His wings doesn't mean that situations won't occur in your life. But our "hope" rests in the notion that God will see us through all trials, and He will not put no more on us than what we can bear.

Jesus Will Never Fail!

Through the gateways of prayer, fasting, mediation on the Word of God, and daily communication with the Lord, the ability to withstand trials and tribulations becomes easier.

James 1:2-3 says to us, "My brethren, count it all joy when ye fall into divers temptations; Knowing this, that the trying of your faith worketh patience." From an outside view, one may frown at the notion the Apostle James spoke of. Taken at face value, how can you bask in a joyous moment when faced with various trials or temptations? The answer is found in the latter end of the second scripture. "…. that the trying of your faith worketh patience."

So what is patience?

❖ the capacity to accept or tolerate delay, trouble, or suffering without getting angry or upset.

That particular virtue is needed when waiting for the manifestation of prayers or declarations unto the Lord. When you're going through situations, it's imperative to rest in patience and continue to trust in the Lord. If I had been impatient while I was in college, I would've abandoned the process and missed the blessing the Lord had waiting for me.

If we were at a staged event, and a microphone was passed around, many could testify of the goodness of the Lord. Standing on the other side of a trial provides undeniable truth that helps our Christian walk of life.

As we embark on another year's journey, life challenges will emerge. In spite of all world events, Jesus is Lord! Take a moment and allow those words to echo in the borders of your soul. When you consider the characteristics that encompass "Lord" you will discover an unending concern of compassion.

He is concerned about what concerns us!

Whatever situations we experience cannot alter His love toward His creations. He paid the ultimate price by offering His body as a ransom, the lamb slain before the foundation of the world.

Isaiah 53:5 says, "But he was wounded for our transgressions, he was bruised for our iniquities: the chastisement of our peace was upon him; and with his stripes we are healed."

He demonstrated His love and took our place on the cross. And when He rose, all power was given until Him. So there's nothing that we can go through that can separate us from His love. His compassion is beyond lip service. I've encountered several experiences, but one thing is for sure: Jesus will never fail.

His love never wavered.

His grace and mercy are everlasting.

What I've learned through trials and tribulations is that **Jesus Will Never Fail.**

Romans 8: 35-39
Who shall separate us from the love of Christ? Shall tribulation, or distress, or persecution, or famine, or nakedness, or peril, or sword?
As it is written, For thy sake we are killed all the day long; we are accounted as sheep for the slaughter.
Nay, in all these things we are more than conquerors through him that loved us.
For I am persuaded, that neither death, nor life, nor angels, nor principalities, nor powers, nor things present, nor things to come,
Nor height, nor depth, nor any other creature, shall be able to separate us from the love of God, which is in Christ Jesus our Lord.

Strength Beyond Trials
by Minister Denise Lamar

Whew……the scripture says that trials come to make us strong. Well, I am STRONG. The trials I have gone through have developed me into the person I am today. I have learned to appreciate the small things in life because they have become my foundation. Through many toils and snares I have overcome, and those times were not easy, but I learned to be strong. James 1:2 says, "Count it all joy when you fall into divers temptations (trials). However, when going through troubling times, we don't feel joyful, and sometimes, you just want to give up. But I thank God for my tribe who always remind me that I have come to far now to look back. We fall down, but we know FAILURE IS NOT AN OPTION. So, through every trial, we fight!

Trials have taught me patience, longsuffering, and faith. I have learned, and I am still learning, how to wait on God.

Patience is a virtue even during the times when the trial you are in seems like it will never end. It is during times like this where you learn longsuffering. As a child, I heard the elderly saints say, "Go through the trial with prayer and fasting and patience because if you don't pass it, you will have to go through it again". I never understood what those words meant until I found myself being tested with the same trial again and again. Sometimes, we find ourselves stuck in the same situation because we have not yet learned how to overcome. Now, I have learned to examine myself in the trial to make sure I am learning from the experience so that I am always victorious. My faith says I am an overcomer and that whatever trial comes my way I will win.

1 Peter 5:10 says, "The God of all grace who hath called us unto his eternal glory by Christ Jesus after that you have suffered a while make you perfect, stablish, strengthen and settle you."

I have learned that after you have gone through, you come out as pure gold, stronger in faith, and much smarter if you paid attention through the trial.

You gain a stronger love for Christ after each trial because you recognize and know He could bring you through it. He will establish you in your faith and for believing in Him all things because you know He will bring you out.

Lesson Learned
by Kanonta Haynes

There are so many things that I could tell you from the many experiences that I encountered in my spiritual journey. During those experiences, I had to trust God and His Word. There were times when I felt really defeated and weighted down. On several occasions, I cried out to God for help and prayed for Him to take the troubles away.

Prayer and studying the Word were my strength and guide. I had to come to the realization that if I were going to get through my circumstances, I had to rely on God and Hid Word. I could not face them on my own. From the experiences, I learned that it is all right to go through. What I had dealt with was not hurting me, but it was pushing me closer to God.

Every experience is a teachable moment. They teach us how to handle the situations that we face better, the next time we have an encounter with them.

Another thing that I learned was that failure does not count us out. Many times, I failed going through my trials and tribulations, but I never gave up.

When you give up, you have given your circumstances power over you. Also, relying on our own strengths will not help us successfully get through our circumstances. The only way we can get through anything we face is with God. He is our only help.

If I could end this article with a word of encouragement, I would say that no matter how hard your battles get or seem, trust, and know that you will have the victory in the end. Do not give up or give in because as we often say, "Troubles do not last always."

Forgiveness Is Greater
by Christine L. George

As I look back over my life and think about all the trials and tribulations I have endured, the most important thing that I have learned is that forgiveness in greater than unforgiveness. What do I mean by that statement? This means that no matter what people have said or done to me, forgiveness is greater than unforgiveness. God is greater than my situation. God knows all and sees all. He knows what I am going through, what I will go through (Jeremiah 29:11), and I have endured a lot.

I grew up in a home where my father was very abusive to my mother, neglected his role as a father, and while that was going on, I was being molested by my uncle. Years later my sons' biological father was murdered. I have face financial struggles where I had to file bankruptcy.

It took me many years of being angry at myself, bitter, and unforgiving at my father and uncle, to realize that I have wasted time being stuck:

- ❖ Stuck in the time when my life was in total chaos.
- ❖ Stuck in being a little girl trapped in a woman's body.
- ❖ Stuck in bitterness, rejection, abandonment, hate, and anger.

But most of all, I was stick in unforgiveness. I wasted so much time being stuck, that I did not know how to move forward. You are not only stuck in what happened to you, but you're also stuck in the pain and misery of what the abuse and betrayal caused you and what it cost you. Then you have to think about what it cost Jesus. He went through trials and tribulations; people didn't believe Him, people talked about Him, friends turned their backs on Him, friends lied about Him, and people beat Him, but until His death, He forgave them (Luke 23:34). He didn't look back. He looked forward to His higher calling, His true purpose, which was dying on the cross to free us from the bondage of sin.

Philippians 3: 13-14 tell us,"Brethren, I count not myself to have apprehended: but this one thing I do, forgetting those things which are behind, and reaching forth unto those things which are before, I press toward the mark for the prize of the high calling of God in Christ Jesus." As long as we are a believer, trials and tribulations will come, but we can't stay there. We have a higher calling to do God's will. What we are going through or have gone through is not for us to keep to ourselves, but to help someone else through the same situations because God does not waste our pain.

I know you may be reading this article and thinking, "You don't understand what he/she did to me," "That's easy for you to say. I lost everything," "I was just a child," "Forget! How can I forget?" I didn't say forgiving and moving forward were going to be easy, but you can do it if you want too.

Today, make the decision to live free of past childhood trauma, bad financial choices, hate, bitterness, rejection, anger, abandonment, and unforgiveness. Whatever that has caused you to be stuck, break free because God has work for you to do.

Like the song says, *"I am free. Praise the Lord I'm free. No longer bound. No more chains holding me."* Today, commit to no longer live in the past because forgiveness is greater.

What I Learned From My Miscarriage
by Sheena M. Ware

Sometimes as Christians, we see God as a magical figure who is supposed to immediately answer all our questions and grant all our requests. But if that were to be true, we would never truly understand or be able to appreciate God's power to the fullest extent.

At the beginning of the year, I asked God to grow my faith. I made a vision board where I asked God to give me faith over fear, purpose, focus, and restoration of my dreams. I never really thought my year would look like the list on my vision board. Between deaths in my husband's and my extended families, a shocking discovery occurred that shook my entire life, which resulted in the loss of my jobs temporarily in March. I felt like what else could go wrong?

I asked God to please give me something to bring joy back into my life. I became focused. In the gym and starting my new blog, I was gaining happiness again.

Then, I found out that I was seven weeks pregnant. Finally, I could give my son a sibling. I was overwhelmed with gratitude. God had heard me. Nothing could ruin my mood.

One week went by. I was still bubbling with excitement, but then it was paired with nerves because something just doesn't feel right. I called my new doctor, whom I hadn't met, for an appointment because I was bleeding, and the blood flow kept getting heavier. An hour later she was extracting my unborn from my womb. I don't think I have ever experienced pain so deep. Because of Covid-19, I had to be alone at the doctor's office and I don't think I have ever felt so isolated. My body had failed me and the baby that God had blessed me with was called home at eight weeks. October 1st officially became the worst day of my life.

The confusion that followed was swallowing me whole. I had so many questions for God. I have been praying, doing Bible studies, and getting closer to Him, and He let this happen to me? I questioned what I had done wrong. I analyzed my every move during the two months prior. Nothing made sense. And God was silent.

I thought about my prayers to God when I first started sensing something was off. "God, please just don't let me lose this child. This is all I have been wanting. I trust you will fulfill my requests." I never once asked God to be with me and guide me through whatever His purpose was.

After the miscarriage, I put on the mask. I went back to work the very next day. I continued enduring physical and mental anguish. I struggled and doubted God. I had so many wonderful people in my life, who came through and gave my soul so much comfort. Their presence was probably the best thing that ever could've happened to me.

I had a moment with God.

I cried to Him, and He reminded me of Jeremiah 29:11- "For I know the plans I have for you, declares the Lord, plans to prosper you and not to harm you, plans to give you hope and a future."

He was actually thinking of me?

In that moment, as I remembered and felt the loneliness of the day I miscarried all over again, Joshua 1:9 entered my spirit. "Have I not commanded you? Be strong and courageous. Do not be afraid; do not be discouraged, for the Lord your God will be with you wherever you go."

Upon reflection, my husband was with me, texting back with quick responses from work. If you know him, you know that quick responses are not his thing. My mom, who drove me to the doctor, never left the parking lot even though she wanted to be in the room with me. She kept my son busy. The doctor, whom I had never met before, was kind and gentle to me, even though I was a complete stranger to her. With compassion, she embraced me through my tears. She gave me time to soak in what had just happened, and dealt with me in the most patient way. Later, when I was home, my sister called and friends flocked to my side to check in on me. They still do.

Even in that room, God was with me. I was never ever alone. God was the silent teacher watching over me as I went through one of the hardest tests I had ever taken in my life.

My miscarriage taught me that God is God, and that's it. He is in control. When I was praying to Him, I was demanding what I wanted instead of just resting in His will for my life, no matter how painful it might be. On January 1, I asked God to strengthen my faith, to give me purpose and focus.

And He did. But wasn't the way I wanted it to happen. I leaned into God and realized that I had cut Him out of my plans. I was making my own ideas of what success should look like and ignoring His plans that were way bigger than mine could've ever been. I learned that faith is easier said than done, but in a relationship with God, it is essential to practice it.

I have days where I slip up and doubt God and what His purpose could possibly be for me, in the midst of this very painful year. I still have emotions to work through because I am human, and that's ok. Even through this learning process, God's footprints are next to mine in the sand.

God's Faithfulness
by Linda G. Pugh, MS, NCC, LAPC

1 I think the greatest lesson I've learned over the last two years of trials and tribulations is that God is truly faithful to keep His promises. He absolutely cannot lie! I've always known that He would never leave nor forsake me, but it has finally taken root in my spirit. After six deaths in my family, including and the passing of both of my parents in 2019, I didn't think I would ever stop crying or get through another day. I didn't know if I would be okay or how I was going to get through such deep agony, grief, and pain, but God kept reminding me that He would never let go of me. I still experience waves of grief, but I know that God is always present.

I understand that my life will never be the same again without my parents and other family members, but I have adjusted my way of thinking, and I find something to be grateful for each day. This mindset helps me to remain in a constant state of gratitude and appreciation for life and legacy. At the end of the day, no matter what adversity I face, I know that I am never alone… God is in it with me every step of the way! Through grief and loss, I have grown more intimate with God and I have learned the value of being in His presence each day. This is where I find the joy that the world cannot give and peace that surpasses all understanding and contentment with the life I have been afforded by the grace of God!

2 I have also learned through painful trials that I cannot control the choices that another person makes. We enter relationships with such high expectations that there will be a good outcome, but we do not have control over what someone else will do to affect that expected outcome. For instance, we go into business or marital relationships with high expectations of being partners for life. However, if one party decides to leave the business or engage in extramarital affairs, that decision will change the outcome of those relationships.

I've learned that nothing in life is guaranteed… jobs end, relationships fail, loved ones perish, children grow up and leave home, but God will never leave us!

He promised that He wouldn't, and that is the only relationship that is guaranteed in this life. I cannot stop other people from doing what they do because ultimately, what they do is their choice. This freedom of choice goes back to free will. God does not force us to serve Him or love Him or receive His gift of salvation because we are not robots, and He will not force anything upon us. We all have the free will to make our own choices and decisions. However, life isn't about waiting for someone to change; it's about taking responsibility for our own healing and forward progress.

3 I've also learned the power of a changed mind and perspective through difficult trials. We have all experienced the heaviness of anxiety, doubt, and uncertainty due to Covid-19. Fear has gripped the hearts of many. Although we cannot control what happens to us, we can control how we respond to it. Thus, we must learn to see things from a different vantage point because living in this heavy state for extended periods of time can result in the prefrontal cortex in the brain shutting down. When this happens, our ability to resolve problems, think logically, or pay attention is impaired. This state increases our chances

of having irrational behaviors, and it makes us prone to anxiety, depression, and stress.

What I've learned to do during this shut-in time is to get still and become more aware of God's presence and His promises.

I have also started journaling my feelings and emotions honestly. My mind is transformed as I give my concerns to God and replace my worries with His promises. Instead of allowing the negative thoughts to take over, I am declaring the Word of God. For instance, Psalm 46:10 says, "Be still, let go, be calm, relax … and know that I am God! With a different perspective comes a different outcome such as peace, joy, and contentment God has promised me.

4 Another life lesson I've learned from a more recent painful experience is that forgiveness allows our blessings. To forgive is to be set free from the baggage that holds us back. People are human, and they will disappoint us, but God is always the same. He will never let us down. So, during times of discouragement and disappointment, instead of looking to people, I've learned to encourage myself.

I do this by remembering where my help comes from. I go into my secret place to meet with the Holy Spirit, seek God's presence, study His word, engage in praise and worship, sing, and serve.

I've learned that discouragement comes from focusing on the problem more than focusing on God. The goal is to forgive and be free and to maintain my peace by keeping my eyes on the One who is the Prince of Peace. I have forgiven everyone that hurt me, and I've released them to God. I've learned to not give up on people, but to give them up to God because holding on to hurt, anger, and unforgiveness only robs me of my peace and ends in bitterness, and no one is worth that.

5 Not only is forgiveness vitally important, letting go and moving forward is another important life lesson I've learned from painful trials and tribulations. Life is not always going to be smooth sailing, but I do not have to allow other people's poor decisions and bad choices to stick to me and hold me back from the life God has for me. The lesson here is I can be hurt but not held back!

6 I've also learned the importance of praying for myself and the people who hurt me. God showed me that there is no heart too broken that Jesus cannot fix, so it's important to pray for our hearts to be healed. Also, there is no life so shattered that Jesus cannot restore, so we must pray for the offenders to be restored as they turn to Him for help because hurting people hurt people.

The Blessings in the Trials
by Kim P. Carrol

I have learned over the years, that there are areas within ourselves, that will not fully develop without resistance and hardships. It is during the rough times of life that you begin to truly discover who you are, and what you are made of. If life never threw us any curve balls, we would only know and demonstrate a fraction of ourselves.

Trials and tribulations are also a part of the journey on the way to discovering who God is and what He can do in our lives. Trials and tribulations are necessary.

James 1:12 says, "Blessed is the man that endureth temptation: for when he is tried, he shall receive the crown of life, which the Lord hath promised to them that love him."

Not only do our trials and tribulations prove God and us, but they also release spiritual and natural rewards. The rewards are overcoming, gaining strength, and receiving power. And when all is said and done, the "Crown of Life" that God has promised to all who love Him will be given.

James 1: 2-4 tells us, "My brethren, count it all joy when ye fall into divers temptations; Knowing this, that the trying of your faith worketh patience.But let patience have her perfect work, that ye may be perfect and entire, wanting nothing."

Trials and tribulations test us. They test our faith and endurance, so that we can grow and mature. They cause us to be whole and complete, lacking nothing. Consider a precious diamond. If the diamond had not been through the fire and withstood high amounts of pressure, the diamond would not be formed. It would also fail to reach its highest value and reflex light the way it should.

God uses all things to work for the good of those who love Him; those that are called according to His purpose. Even the trials of life are for our good. Therefore, rejoice and be glad when they come, because God is doing his marvelous work in your life.

Perseverance
by Tra'Derrius Robinson

In Galatians 6:9, Paul tells us, "Let us not be weary in well doing, for in due season we shall reap, if we faint not." This scripture speaks so much life into our trials and tribulations.

In this life, we are familiar with spring, summer, fall, and winter. In these seasons changes start to take place throughout the earth. The temperature turns from hot to cold. The leaves that were once on the tree are now on the ground. The grass that once was alive is now dead.

Yes, we have gone through all four seasons but there is one season that believers are waiting to come. That time is our due season, the appointed time by God for your trials and tribulations to become a testimony.

In the year 2020, the world seemed to be in turmoil, but yet I had greater faith through the trials and tribulations of life.

Hellen Keller once said, "Character cannot be developed in ease and quiet. Only through experience of trial and suffering can the soul be strengthened, ambition inspired, and success achieved." This quote reflects the true benefits that I've learned in life. I've learned that trouble truly doesn't last always. The Bible tells us in Psalms 30:5, "That weeping may endure for a night, but joy cometh in the morning."

As a pandemic—college student, there are times when I felt like things would not get better. I cried and pleaded unto God that He would keep my mind in perfect piece. Sometimes, it seemed like my prayers never touched heaven. But yet when the time was right, my due season came. As I made it through that season, things changed abruptly to another season of dealing with the spirit of depression. Yet in my depression, I found inspiration to start my own business. There I was again, my due season had come.

I went through depression in order for my mind, my heart, and my soul to be strengthened. In my due season, those trials and tribulations had been turned into inspiration.

As we move forward in the year 2021, I'm expecting a season of success. I've learned that if you truly sow yourself to righteousness, you will reap in mercy.

I encourage you to take that trial and tribulation as a blessing because due season is soon to come.

I've learned so much while enduring trials and tribulations. I encourage you to hold true to God's word, for it never changes; instead, it feeds our heart and souls to change our lives. I leave you with this scripture.

2 Corinthians 4:8-9 says, "We are troubled on every side, yet not distressed; we are perplexed, but not in despair; Persecuted, but not forsaken; cast down, but not destroyed."

Purpose with a plan
by Que Nona Guilford

God has us on this earth for a reason and we waste so much time trying to find it. Storms come and go, but our purpose will always be with us. We must hold onto God's promise and His Plan for our life. Change your perspective and allow your storm to produce your purpose. God is in control of our life, if we give Him excess. All God ask us to do is our best. Yes, life can give us challenges, but we can use them for our purpose. Before we were in our mother's womb, God had chosen our purpose. He knew that we would have the obstacles in our life. He placed them in our lives to help produce our purpose.

For example, I was raped, molested, abandon, mistreated, rejected and so much more but these moments don't define or stop me from my purpose. These moments are a piece of me. They were moments that hurt me;

however, they walked me into my purpose.

God allows somethings to hit our lives, to help somebody else. I wouldn't be a domestic violence advocate if I hadn't faced it myself. Finding your purpose is not easy, but it is necessary. The pain of situations can help develop a new mind and perspective of things. I can't tell you to keep pushing no matter what people say or do if I hadn't been through rejection or mistreated.

Don't allow your past to stop your future. Let it make your future. You have so much more to live for. You can't give up because it was necessary for you to make it. Stop fighting the process and allow God to change your perspective of your purpose. He has so much planned for you and designed for you to walk-in. He has already gifted you with the anointing for your journey. You must position yourself so that God can develop you. He will send you help to equipment you for your journey.

He knows your strength and weaknesses. Why do you think God saved and protect you from all that danger? Yes, He allows somethings to happen so you can understand other people.

- ❖ Will you die with the river in your belly?
- ❖ What does God have to do to get your attention?
- ❖ When will you be self-motivated and trust him on this journey?

You have been anointed and the world needs it. The favor of God is in your mouth. Will you allow God to take you through the process and prepare you for the next generation?

Trust the Process
by Kim J. McKinney

In this life(world), we will have tribulation. What is tribulation? To give my personal definition, it means "trouble."

According to Merriam-Webster Dictionary, tribulation means distress or suffering from oppression or persecution. Affliction, distress, pain.

I'm quite sure we all have experienced trouble, pain, and/or distress at some point in our lives. In John 16:33, Jesus had already prepared us for such a thing. So tribulation comes as no surprise, although we are surprised, shocked, and in disbelief when bad things happen to us in life.

Jesus told us to not worry when we experience tribulation; because He overcame, and we have the same choice as well. Overcome. Is it easy? For me, it was not easy sometimes when I faced with trials and tribulations.

In some instances they were based on what I faced—lies, betrayal, loss of a loved one, divorce, children going astray, and various other events. Some of them I had gone through all at the same time, which seemed to be overwhelming and I felt like my faith was being put on trial, and tested.

According to Macmillan Dictionary, a trial is the process of testing products or pain; painful or difficult experience.

During these times, I wanted to give up and give in. I cried, cried, and cried some more. I didn't see anything getting better. I prayed and nothing happened. I grew weary. As much of the Word that I have in me, there were times I couldn't open my mouth to release it because the magnitude of what I experienced was too overwhelming. I felt like Job, as one thing after another, made its way into my life.

Have anyone ever faced something back to back, as if you couldn't catch a break? The songwriter said, "I won't complain. I could, but I won't." Well guess what, I didn't always pass the test. I complained, I whined, and I felt sorry for myself. And I cried some more.

One day, during my quiet alone time, I heard the Spirit of the Lord say, "Worship Me. Minister to Me with your worship." As I worshipped Him, I started feeling relieved. Although things had not changed or gotten better, I kept worshipping Him. I started giving God praise and adoration. Not that I didn't already know or give God praise and adoration, but my trials, tests, and the tribulations, allowed me to become distracted, distressed, and unfocused.

Thanks be unto God, for not giving up on me. Proverbs 13: 13 says, "Hope deferred, makes the heart sick." What I was hoping for wasn't manifesting fast enough.

According to Romans 5:3-4 And not only so, but we glory in tribulations also: knowing that tribulation worketh patience; And patience, experience; and experience, hope:

What I was going through, was working something far greater in me, than I could see. Because I wasn't seeing what I was praying for manifesting right then, I grew and learned to be patient. I experienced another level of Worship while I was waiting.

Then, I had to go on a fast at different times, because what I was going through was not going to move except by fasting and praying. Isaiah 58: 6 says, "Is not this the fast that I have chosen? to loose the bands of wickedness, to undo the heavy burdens, and to let the oppressed go free, and that ye and that ye break every yoke?"

During and after I fasted, I saw a breakthrough. I saw manifestation of what I believed God for. Because I'm called according to His purpose, the trials and tribulations that I was going through started working for my good.

What the enemy meant for evil, God turned it around in my favor. He gave me unspeakable joy. My faith was no longer wavering; it increased. My communication to God intensified, and I experienced spiritual growth. My perspective and perception changed. Through it all, I learned to trust the process. I gained maturity and wisdom, and I learned to trust God totally without reservation. During the experience, knowledge and strategies on how to minster were learned.

Some trials are necessary to bring you to another level for the next assignment in your life. You won't understand everything at all times.

But after the rain and storms of life, the Son broke through, and I even saw a rainbow, which reminded me of the Covenant that I had with the Father. No matter what, He would never leave me, nor forsake Me. He was there all the time. He is there with you all the time. Trust Him and surrender to His divine will.

About the Author

T.K. Ware's style of writing brings a fresh perspective of faith-based books, in which he calls, Suspense with Soul. His inspired writings weave together reality with the supernatural, in hope to plant a seed of the gospel. Often known for his memorable fictional characters and series, including Charles "ESQUIRE" Everson, The Pastor's Daughter, Ebony's Confessions, If I Could: A Son's Plea, and the Up Close & Personal Series. Outside of fictional writing, he employs inspiration and motivation through his devotionals.

Learn more at www.insightfulcp.com

Journal Entries

Write the vision and make it plain….

Habakkuk 2:2-3

And the Lord answered me, and said, Write the vision, and make it plain upon tables, that he may run that readeth it.

For the vision is yet for an appointed time, but at the end it shall speak, and not lie: though it tarry, wait for it; because it will surely come, it will not tarry.

What brings you joy?

Considering everything that happened last year, what do you hope to accomplish this year?

_____
_____
_____
_____
_____
_____
_____
_____
_____
_____
_____
_____
_____
_____
_____

Which areas do you need to improve in with your relationship with the Lord?

_____

_____

_____

_____

_____

_____

_____

_____

_____

_____

_____

_____

_____

What are you grateful for?

List your goals, dreams, and desires?

SCRIPTURES FOR MEDITAITON

Psalm 37:4-5
Delight thyself also in the Lord: and he shall give thee the desires of thine heart.
Commit thy way unto the Lord; trust also in him; and he shall bring it to pass.

1 John 5:14-15
And this is the confidence that we have in him, that, if we ask any thing according to his will, he heareth us:
And if we know that he hear us, whatsoever we ask, we know that we have the petitions that we desired of him.

John 15:7
If ye abide in me, and my words abide in you, ye shall ask what ye will, and it shall be done unto you.

THE NAMES OF JESUS

Everything you need is wrapped up in JESUS. Learn of Him and embrace the holiness of His glory.

- ❖ ADAM: (1 Corinthians 15:45) And so it is written, The first man Adam was made a living soul; the last Adam was made a quickening spirit.

- ❖ ADVOCATE: (1 John 2:1) My little children, these things write I unto you, that ye sin not. And if any man sin, we have an advocate with the Father, Jesus Christ the righteous:

- ❖ ALMIGHTY: (Revelation 1:8) I am Alpha and Omega, the beginning and the ending, saith the Lord, which is, and which was, and which is to come, the Almighty.

- ❖ ALPHA AND OMEGA: (Revelation 1:8) I am Alpha and Omega, the beginning and the ending, saith the Lord, which is, and which was, and which is to come, the Almighty.

- ❖ AMEN: (Revelation 3:14) And unto the angel of the church of the Laodiceans write; These things saith the Amen, the faithful and true witness, the beginning of the creation of God;

- ❖ APOSTLE OF OUR PROFESSION: (Hebrews 3:1) Wherefore, holy brethren, partakers of the heavenly calling, consider the Apostle and High Priest of our profession, Christ Jesus;

- ❖ ARM OF THE LORD: (Isaiah 51:9) Awake, awake, put on strength, O arm of the LORD; awake, as in the ancient days, in the generations of old. Art thou not it that hath cut Rahab, and wounded the dragon?

- ❖ (Isaiah 53:1) Who hath believed our report? and to whom is the arm of the LORD revealed?

- ❖ AUTHOR AND FINISHER OF OUR FAITH: (Hebrews 12:2) Looking unto Jesus the author and finisher of our faith; who for the joy that was set before him endured the cross, despising the shame, and is set down at the right hand of the throne of God.

- ❖ AUTHOR OF ETERNAL SALVATION: (Hebrews 5:9) And being made perfect, he became the author of eternal salvation unto all them that obey him;

- ❖ BEGINNING OF CREATION OF GOD: (Revelation 3:14) And unto the angel of the church of the Laodiceans write; These things saith the Amen, the faithful and true witness, the beginning of the creation of God;

- ❖ BELOVED SON: (Matthew 12:18) Behold my servant, whom I have chosen; my beloved, in whom my soul is well pleased: I will put my spirit upon him, and he shall show judgment to the Gentiles.

- ❖ BLESSED AND ONLY POTENTATE: (1 Timothy 6:15) Which in his times he shall show, who is the blessed and only Potentate, the King of kings, and Lord of lords;

- ❖ BRANCH: (Isaiah 4:2) In that day shall the branch of the LORD be beautiful and glorious, and the fruit of the earth shall be excellent and comely for them that are escaped of Israel.

- ❖ BREAD OF LIFE: (John 6:32) Then Jesus said unto them, Verily, verily, I say unto you, Moses gave you not that bread from heaven; but my Father giveth you the true bread from heaven.

- ❖ CAPTAIN OF SALVATION: (Hebrews 2:10) For it became him, for whom are all things, and by whom are all things, in bringing many sons unto glory, to make the captain of their salvation perfect through sufferings.

- ❖ CHIEF SHEPHERD: (1 Peter 5:4) And when the chief Shepherd shall appear, ye shall receive a crown of glory that fadeth not away.

- ❖ CHRIST OF GOD: (Luke 9:20) He said unto them, But whom say ye that I am? Peter answering said, The Christ of God.

- ❖ CONSOLATION OF ISRAEL: (Luke 2:25) And, behold, there was a man in Jerusalem, whose name was Simeon; and the same man was just and devout, waiting for the consolation of Israel: and the Holy Ghost was upon him.

- ❖ CORNERSTONE: (Psalm 118:22) The stone which the builders refused is become the head stone of the corner.

- ❖ COUNSELLOR: (Isaiah 9:6) For unto us a child is born, unto us a son is given: and the government shall be upon his shoulder: and his name shall be called Wonderful, Counsellor, The mighty God, The everlasting Father, The Prince of Peace.

- ❖ CREATOR: (John 1:3) All things were made by him; and without him was not any thing made that was made.

- ❖ DAYSPRING: (Luke 1:78) Through the tender mercy of our God; whereby the dayspring from on high hath visited us,

- ❖ DELIVERER: (Romans 11:26) And so all Israel shall be saved: as it is written, There shall come out of Zion the Deliverer, and shall turn away ungodliness from Jacob:

- ❖ DESIRE OF THE NATIONS: (Haggai 2:7) And I will shake all nations, and the desire of all nations shall come: and I will fill this house with glory, saith the LORD of hosts.

- ❖ DOOR: (John 10:7) Then said Jesus unto them again, Verily, verily, I say unto you, I am the door of the sheep.

- ❖ ELECT OF GOD: (Isaiah 42:1) Behold my servant, whom I uphold; mine elect, in whom my soul delighteth; I have put my spirit upon him: he shall bring forth judgment to the Gentiles.

- ❖ EVERLASTING FATHER: (Isaiah 9:6) For unto us a child is born, unto us a son is given: and the government shall be upon his shoulder: and his name shall be called Wonderful, Counsellor, The mighty God, The everlasting Father, The Prince of Peace.

- ❖ FAITHFUL WITNESS: (Revelation 1:5) And from Jesus Christ, who is the faithful witness, and the first begotten of the dead, and the prince of the kings of the earth. Unto him that loved us, and washed us from our sins in his own blood,

- ❖ FIRST AND LAST: (Revelation 1:17) And when I saw him, I fell at his feet as dead. And he laid his right hand upon me, saying unto me, Fear not; I am the first and the last:

- ❖ FIRST BEGOTTEN: (Revelation 1:5) And from Jesus Christ, who is the faithful witness, and the first begotten of the dead, and the prince of the kings of the earth. Unto him that loved us, and washed us from our sins in his own blood,

- ❖ FORERUNNER: (Hebrews 6:20) Whither the forerunner is for us entered, even Jesus, made an high priest for ever after the order of Melchisedec.

- ❖ GLORY OF THE LORD: (Isaiah 40:5) And the glory of the LORD shall be revealed, and all flesh shall see it together: for the mouth of the LORD hath spoken it.

- ❖ GOD: (Isaiah 40:3) The voice of him that crieth in the wilderness, Prepare ye the way of the LORD, make straight in the desert a highway for our God.

- ❖ GOD BLESSED: (Romans 9:5) Whose are the fathers, and of whom as concerning the flesh Christ came, who is over all, God blessed for ever. Amen.

- ❖ GOOD SHEPHERD: (John 10:11) I am the good shepherd: the good shepherd giveth his life for the sheep.

- ❖ GOVERNOR: (Matthew 2:6) And thou Bethlehem, in the land of Juda, art not the least among the princes of Juda: for out of thee shall come a Governor, that shall rule my people Israel.

- ❖ GREAT HIGH PRIEST: (Hebrews 4:14) Seeing then that we have a great high priest, that is passed into the heavens, Jesus the Son of God, let us hold fast our profession.

- ❖ HEAD OF THE CHURCH: (Ephesians 1:22) And hath put all things under his feet, and gave him to be the head over all things to the church,

- ❖ HEIR OF ALL THINGS: (Hebrews 1:2) Hath in these last days spoken unto us by his Son, whom he hath appointed heir of all things, by whom also he made the worlds;

- ❖ HOLY CHILD: (Acts 4:27) For of a truth against thy holy child Jesus, whom thou hast anointed, both Herod, and Pontius Pilate, with the Gentiles, and the people of Israel, were gathered together,

- ❖ HOLY ONE: (Acts 3:14) But ye denied the Holy One and the Just, and desired a murderer to be granted unto you;

- ❖ HOLY ONE OF GOD: (Mark 1:24) Saying, Let us alone; what have we to do with thee, thou Jesus of Nazareth? art thou come to destroy us? I know thee who thou art, the Holy One of God.

- ❖ HOLY ONE OF ISRAEL: (Isaiah 41:14) Fear not, thou worm Jacob, and ye men of Israel; I will help thee, saith the LORD, and thy redeemer, the Holy One of Israel.

- ❖ HORN OF SALVATION: (Luke 1:69) And hath raised up an horn of salvation for us in the house of his servant David;

- ❖ I AM: (John 8:58) Jesus said unto them, Verily, verily, I say unto you, Before Abraham was, I am.

- ❖ JESUS OF NAZARETH: (Matthew 21:11) And the multitude said, This is Jesus the prophet of Nazareth of Galilee.

- ❖ IMAGE OF GOD: (2 Corinthians 4:4) In whom the god of this world hath blinded the minds of them which believe not, lest the light of the glorious gospel of Christ, who is the image of God, should shine unto them.

- ❖ IMMANUEL: (Isaiah 7:14) Therefore the Lord himself shall give you a sign; Behold, a virgin shall conceive, and bear a son, and shall call his name Immanuel.

- ❖ JEHOVAH: (Isaiah 26:4) Trust ye in the LORD for ever: for in the LORD JEHOVAH is everlasting strength:

- ❖ JESUS: (Matthew 1:21) And she shall bring forth a son, and thou shalt call his name JESUS: for he shall save his people from their sins.

- ❖ JUDGE OF ISRAEL: (Micah 5:1) Now gather thyself in troops, O daughter of troops: he hath laid siege against us: they shall smite the judge of Israel with a rod upon the cheek.

- ❖ THE JUST ONE: (Acts 7:52) Which of the prophets have not your fathers persecuted? and they have slain them which showed before of the coming of the Just One; of whom ye have been now the betrayers and murderers:

- ❖ KING: (Zechariah 9:9) Rejoice greatly, O daughter of Zion; shout, O daughter of Jerusalem: behold, thy King cometh unto thee: he is just, and having salvation; lowly, and riding upon an ass, and upon a colt the foal of an ass.

- ❖ KING OF THE AGES: (1 Timothy 1:17) Now unto the King eternal, immortal, invisible, the only wise God, be honour and glory for ever and ever. Amen.

- ❖ KING OF THE JEWS: (Matthew 2:2) Saying, Where is he that is born King of the Jews? for we have seen his star in the east, and are come to worship him.

- ❖ KING OF KINGS: (1 Timothy 6:15) Which in his times he shall show, who is the blessed and only Potentate, the King of kings, and Lord of lords;

- ❖ KING OF SAINTS: (Revelation 15:3) And they sing the song of Moses the servant of God, and the song of the Lamb, saying, Great and marvellous are thy works, Lord God Almighty; just and true are thy ways, thou King of saints.

- ❖ LAWGIVER: (Isaiah 33:22) For the LORD is our judge, the LORD is our lawgiver, the LORD is our king; he will save us.

- ❖ LAMB: (Revelation 13:8) And all that dwell upon the earth shall worship him, whose names are not written in the book of life of the Lamb slain from the foundation of the world.

- ❖ THE LAMB OF GOD: (John 1:29) The next day John seeth Jesus coming unto him, and saith, Behold the Lamb of God, which taketh away the sin of the world.

- ❖ THE LEADER AND COMMANDER: (Isaiah 55:4) Behold, I have given him for a witness to the people, a leader and commander to the people.

- ❖ THE WAY, TRUTH, AND THE LIFE: (John 14:6) Jesus saith unto him, I am the way, the truth, and the life: no man cometh unto the Father, but by me.

- ❖ LIGHT OF THE WORLD: (John 8:12) Then spake Jesus again unto them, saying, I am the light of the world: he that followeth me shall not walk in darkness, but shall have the light of life.

- ❖ LION OF THE TRIBE OF JUDAH: (Revelation 5:5) And one of the elders saith unto me, Weep not: behold, the Lion of the tribe of Juda, the Root of David, hath prevailed to open the book, and to loose the seven seals thereof.

- ❖ LORD OF ALL: (Acts 10:36) The word which God sent unto the children of Israel, preaching peace by Jesus Christ: (he is Lord of all:)

- ❖ LORD OF GLORY: (1 Corinthians 2:8) Which none of the princes of this world knew: for had they known it, they would not have crucified the Lord of glory.

- ❖ LORD OF LORDS: (1 Timothy 6:15) Which in his times he shall show, who is the blessed and only Potentate, the King of kings, and Lord of lords;

- ❖ LORD OF OUR RIGHTEOUSNESS: (Jeremiah 23:6) In his days Judah shall be saved, and Israel shall dwell safely: and this is his name whereby he shall be called, THE LORD OUR RIGHTEOUSNESS.

- ❖ THE MAN OF SORROWS: (Isaiah 53:3) He is despised and rejected of men; a man of sorrows, and acquainted with grief: and we hid as it were our faces from him; he was despised, and we esteemed him not.

- ❖ THE MEDIATOR: (1 Timothy 2:5) For there is one God, and one mediator between God and men, the man Christ Jesus;

- ❖ MESSENGER OF THE COVENANT: (Malachi 3:1) Behold, I will send my messenger, and he shall prepare the way before me: and the Lord, whom ye seek, shall suddenly come to his temple, even the messenger of the covenant, whom ye delight in: behold, he shall come, saith the LORD of hosts.

- ❖ MESSIAH: (Daniel 9:25) Know therefore and understand, that from the going forth of the commandment to restore and to build Jerusalem unto the Messiah the Prince shall be seven weeks, and threescore and two weeks: the street shall be built again, and the wall, even in troublous times.

- ❖ (John 1:41) He first findeth his own brother Simon, and saith unto him, We have found the Messiah, which is, being interpreted, the Christ.

- ❖ MIGHTY GOD: (Isaiah 9:6) For unto us a child is born, unto us a son is given: and the government shall be upon his shoulder: and his name shall be called Wonderful, Counsellor, The mighty God, The everlasting Father, The Prince of Peace.

- ❖ MIGHTY ONE: (Isaiah 60:16) Thou shalt also suck the milk of the Gentiles, and shalt suck the breast of kings: and thou shalt know that I the LORD am thy Saviour and thy Redeemer, the mighty One of Jacob.

- ❖ MORNING STAR: (Revelation 22:16) I Jesus have sent mine angel to testify unto you these things in the churches. I am the root and the offspring of David, and the bright and morning star.

- ❖ NAZARENE: (Matthew 2:23) And he came and dwelt in a city called Nazareth: that it might be fulfilled which was spoken by the prophets, He shall be called a Nazarene.

- ❖ ONLY BEGOTTEN SON: (John 1:18) No man hath seen God at any time; the only begotten Son, which is in the bosom of the Father, he hath declared him.

- ❖ OUR PASSOVER: (1 Corinthians 5:7) Purge out therefore the old leaven, that ye may be a new lump, as ye are unleavened. For even Christ our passover is sacrificed for us:

- ❖ PRINCE OF LIFE: (Acts 3:15) And killed the Prince of life, whom God hath raised from the dead; whereof we are witnesses.

- ❖ **PRINCE OF KINGS:** (Revelation 1:5) And from Jesus Christ, who is the faithful witness, and the first begotten of the dead, and the prince of the kings of the earth. Unto him that loved us, and washed us from our sins in his own blood,

- ❖ **PRINCE OF PEACE:** (Isaiah 9:6) For unto us a child is born, unto us a son is given: and the government shall be upon his shoulder: and his name shall be called Wonderful, Counsellor, The mighty God, The everlasting Father, The Prince of Peace.

- ❖ **PROPHET:** (Luke 24:19) And he said unto them, What things? And they said unto him, Concerning Jesus of Nazareth, which was a prophet mighty in deed and word before God and all the people:

- ❖ (Acts 3:22) For Moses truly said unto the fathers, A prophet shall the Lord your God raise up unto you of your brethren, like unto me; him shall ye hear in all things whatsoever he shall say unto you.

- ❖ **REDEEMER:** (Job 19:25) For I know that my redeemer liveth, and that he shall stand at the latter day upon the earth:

- ❖ **RESURRECTION AND LIFE:** (John 11:25) Jesus said unto her, I am the resurrection, and the life: he that believeth in me, though he were dead, yet shall he live:

- ❖ ROCK: (1 Corinthians 10:4) And did all drink the same spiritual drink: for they drank of that spiritual Rock that followed them: and that Rock was Christ.

- ❖ ROOT OF DAVID: (Revelation 22:16) I Jesus have sent mine angel to testify unto you these things in the churches. I am the root and the offspring of David, and the bright and morning star.

- ❖ ROSE OF SHARON: (Song of Songs 2:1) I am the rose of Sharon, and the lily of the valleys.

- ❖ SAVIOR: (Luke 2:11) For unto you is born this day in the city of David a Saviour, which is Christ the Lord.

- ❖ SEED OF WOMAN: (Genesis 3:15) And I will put enmity between thee and the woman, and between thy seed and her seed; it shall bruise thy head, and thou shalt bruise his heel.

- ❖ SHEPHERD AND BISHOP OF SOULS: (1 Peter 2:25) For ye were as sheep going astray; but are now returned unto the Shepherd and Bishop of your souls.

- ❖ SHILOH: (Genesis 49:10) The sceptre shall not depart from Judah, nor a lawgiver from between his feet, until Shiloh come; and unto him shall the gathering of the people be.

- ❖ SON OF THE BLESSED: (Mark 14:61) But he held his peace, and answered nothing. Again the high priest asked him, and said unto him, Art thou the Christ, the Son of the Blessed?

- ❖ SON OF DAVID: (Matthew 1:1) The book of the generation of Jesus Christ, the son of David, the son of Abraham.

- ❖ SON OF GOD: (Matthew 2:15) And was there until the death of Herod: that it might be fulfilled which was spoken of the Lord by the prophet, saying, Out of Egypt have I called my son.

- ❖ SON OF THE HIGHEST: (Luke 1:32) He shall be great, and shall be called the Son of the Highest: and the Lord God shall give unto him the throne of his father David:

- ❖ SUN OF RIGHTEOUSNESS:
  (Malachi 4:2) But unto you that fear my name shall the Sun of righteousness arise with healing in his wings; and ye shall go forth, and grow up as calves of the stall.

- ❖ TRUE LIGHT: (John 1:9) That was the true Light, which lighteth every man that cometh into the world.

- ❖ TRUE VINE: (John 15:1) I am the true vine, and my Father is the husbandman.

- ❖ TRUTH: (John 1:14) And the Word was made flesh, and dwelt among us, (and we beheld his glory, the glory as of the only begotten of the Father,) full of grace and truth.

- ❖ WITNESS: (Isaiah 55:4) Behold, I have given him for a witness to the people, a leader and commander to the people.

- ❖ THE WORD: (John 1:1) In the beginning was the Word, and the Word was with God, and the Word was God.

- ❖ THE WORD OF GOD: (Revelation 19:13) And he was clothed with a vesture dipped in blood: and his name is called The Word of God.

VISION THE EYES OF A POET

Visit The Website To Pre Order This Divinely Written Book Of Poetic Expressions
www.insightfulcp.com

Positioning For The Future

As we ponder on the past, present, and future
One must take into consideration the destiny
We endure trials and tribulations
And oftentimes are stagnant with limitations of doubt

We've crossed the waters of pandemic
And the dry land is still not present
It's lingering like a fog hoovering above the waters
So many have drowned and are still drowning

Faith, that exists in many
Has been attacked by the fear of the unknown
So their destiny fades away in the fog of circumstances
And yet, they pray in fear and hope in fear

So when will the cycle end?
Fear is growing daily in alarming numbers
As the "faith" of the pillars of hope are leaving the scene
The enteral time clock is entering the final hour

Now is the time, to seek the Lord wholeheartedly
The climate is shifting for the Ancient of Days
He that hath an ear to hear,
Let him perceive what is said

Get your spiritual houses in order
Visitations are nigh
Regardless of the circumstances that surround you
Pause and consider your past, present, and future

God was here before the foundations of the world
Everything is subject to His Sovereignty
He knew you by name before you were formed
And His angels come to your aid when faith is ignited

So where do we go from here?
As fear swarm like killer bees
The Psalmist wrote, "He that dwelleth in the secret place of the most High shall abide under the shadow of the Almighty. I will say of the LORD, He is my refuge and my fortress: my God; in him with trust."
The solution was written before we were born
So stand in faith and be planted as a tree

For what's coming upon the face of the earth
It's critical to abide in the presence of the Lord
He knows the beginning and ending of all things
And has a path of expectation
For those who will abide and call upon His name

www.ingramcontent.com/pod-product-compliance
Lightning Source LLC
Chambersburg PA
CBHW071235090426
42736CB00014B/3086